BRITAIN'S HERITAGE

London Buses

Oliver Green

AMBERLEY

Acknowledgements

All photographs in this book are from the collection of London Transport Museum/Transport for London (except p.31 Oliver Green, p.32 Mike Sutcliffe, p.40 John F. Stiles, p.58 Wikipedia commons; p.61 (both), p.62 Oliver Green).
Cover image: A conductor wearing a Gibson ticket machine standing beside a Routemaster bus at Chiswick Training School, c. 1973.

About the Author

Oliver Green is a museums consultant, historian and lecturer. He is the former Head Curator of the London Transport Museum and is now its Research Fellow and a Trustee of the LTM Friends. He has written, edited and contributed to several books on transport, art and design including *Frank Pick's London: Art, Design and the Modern City* (2013), *Rails in the Road, A History of Tramways in the UK and Ireland* (2016) and *London's Underground, the Story of the Tube* (2019) as well as *Art Deco* (2018) in the Britain's Heritage series.

First published 2019

Amberley Publishing
The Hill, Stroud
Gloucestershire, GL5 4EP

www.amberley-books.com

Copyright © Oliver Green, 2019

The right of Oliver Green to be identified as the Author of this work has been asserted in accordance with the Copyrights, Designs and Patents Act 1988.

ISBN 978 1 4456 9103 9 (paperback)
ISBN 978 1 4456 9104 6 (ebook)

British Library Cataloguing in Publication Data.
A catalogue record for this book is available from the British Library.

Typesetting by Aura Technology and Software Services, India. Printed in the UK.

Contents

1
Introduction

The London bus represents a curious paradox. The red double-decker became famous and internationally recognised as a distinctive icon of the city in the 1950s and 1960s. London had more buses than any other city, and they were all custom-designed and built for London's tough working conditions, operated on a huge scale by a single giant organisation. London Transport (LT) was widely recognised as the biggest and best urban public transport authority in the world. Buses were only part of that, but the enormous network supported the framework of Underground services, particularly in London's vast suburbs and country areas. For shorter journeys from home to work or leisure, the bus was unbeatable.

But at the very time that it became a symbol of the city, and its numbers increased, the London bus was under serious threat and passenger numbers were in decline. In the mid-twentieth century, before the private car became a serious challenge to the established life of the city, buses took commuters to work, children to school and shoppers to the high street. When Londoners wanted a weekend or evening trip to the countryside, the cinema or a sporting event, they took the bus. But neither local authorities, town planners nor politicians took appropriate action when it was needed.

Curiously, nobody had a plan to prepare London for the rise of the private car and it nearly destroyed the city in the 1970s and 80s. At the time, it also almost looked like the end of the road for the famous London bus. London Transport was ill-equipped to adapt to changing economic and social conditions, and growing political control at local and national level offered no clear way forward for transport management in the city.

Fortunately, the decline was arrested. Political change, limited road space and growing environmental concerns drove a renaissance of the London bus. The city did not invest in yet more carriageway and parking on the Los Angeles model. Instead, bus priority lanes, cheaper fares and significant investment in environmentally cleaner vehicles succeeded in growing patronage. From an all-time low in the 1990s, bus ridership in London has grown strongly in the last twenty-five years and is back to those high levels of the 1950s.

This book is a brief outline of the roller coaster history of the London bus over nearly 200 years. Throughout the nineteenth century the omnibus progressed slowly and its development was severely restricted by the limitations of horse power. Mechanisation came late to London and the modern motor bus was not the dominant mode of transport until the 1920s. Organisation and control of London's buses was formalised with the creation of London Transport in 1933. Yet within another twenty-five years, and the intervention of a devastating world war, the wisdom of running London's buses as a single giant state industry was also called into question.

Recent development under Transport for London (TfL) in the twenty-first century has been very positive but London's future has always been unpredictable. The same goes for its buses. In 2000 nobody could have bet on the sorry fate of the articulated 'bendy bus' in London or the successful introduction of the New Routemaster. Changing trends and political intervention will no doubt continue to make London's buses distinctive and different just as they seemed on course to become dull, boring and just like buses everywhere else.

2
Omnibus Origins

The first London omnibus appeared in the late 1820s, at a time when the great metropolis was quite compact, but growing rapidly. London was already the largest city in the world by population, with the first census in 1801 recording an estimated one million residents. This had grown to around 1.5 million twenty years later, with most of the resident population crowded into a fairly small central area.

For short journeys in the built-up area, nearly everyone walked or took a hired wherry along or across the River Thames. The narrow streets of the old City of London were often crowded with people, livestock being driven to market and horse-drawn goods wagons, all jostling for road space. There were stagecoaches running in and out of town from inns, but journeys had to be pre-booked and drivers were not allowed to pick up or set down anywhere in the paved areas of the City and Westminster.

Virtually no public transport was available on the streets within the paved and built-up area, known as 'the stones' for public carriage licensing purposes. A limited number of hackney carriages were available for hire. The hackney drivers all needed a licence from the Hackney Carriage Office, which maintained a monopoly and a strict quota system which was only occasionally raised. It was effectively a closed shop.

Only the wealthy could afford to own and run a private carriage or ride around town in a hired hackney or sedan chair. As the city grew in the 1820s, so did the ranks of the middle classes. They began to move out of the centre to live in the more pleasant surroundings of villages on the edge of town. These were rapidly becoming London's early suburbs, places like Clapham, Islington and Hackney. The time was ripe for an entrepreneur to step forward and provide a suitably flexible and affordable means of transport that would suit the lifestyle, and the pocket, of the growing suburban middle classes.

On 4 July 1829, coachbuilder George Shillibeer launched his 'omnibus' service, having seen a similar operation introduced in Paris in 1828. It was basically a 'hail and ride' coach service running on a fixed urban route through the city that passengers could join or leave at any point. Unlike a stagecoach, advance booking was not required and travellers paid a conductor on board. Shillibeer copied the service he had seen in Paris, and even the name. Omnibus, meaning 'for all' in Latin, was simply a fleet name, painted in large yellow letters on the side of Shillibeer's two big green vehicles, which were built in his London workshops in Bury Street, Bloomsbury.

Shillibeer's omnibus did not involve any major development in carriage design. In principle it was nothing more than a box on wheels with seating for about twenty passengers inside. Similar vehicles were already used on short stage services running from London to nearby villages like Greenwich, but these all had to be pre-booked and boarded at the terminus, usually an inn. None of the stagecoaches operated on a 'hail and ride' basis, and this was not allowed anywhere in built-up London.

There was one route on which Shillibeer could demonstrate the merits of a Parisian-style coach service without breaking the law. This was along the New Road from Paddington to

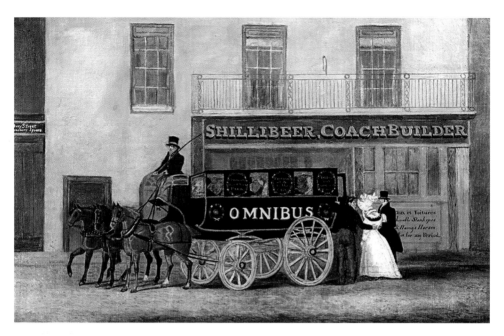

Above: George Shillibeer's original three-horse omnibus outside his Bloomsbury workshop, as it might have looked in 1829. This oil painting is later, but undated.
Below: Shillibeer's advertisement in *The British Traveller* newspaper, 4 July 1829, advertising his omnibus as a fashionable Parisian-style development.

OMNIBUS.

G. SHILLIBEER, induced by the universal admiration the above Vehicles called forth at Paris, has commenced running one upon the Parisian mode, from **PADDINGTON to the BANK.**

The superiority of this Carriage over the ordinary Stage Coaches, for comfort and safety, must be obvious, all the Passengers being Inside, and the Fare charged from Paddington to the Bank being One Shilling, and from Islington to the Bank or Paddington, only Sixpence.

The Proprietor begs to add, that a person of great respectability attends his Vehicle as Conductor; and every possible attention will be paid to the accommodation of Ladies and Children.

Hours of Starting :—From Paddington Green to the Bank, at 9, 12, 3, 6, and 8 o'clock ; from the Bank to Paddington, at 10, 1, 4, 7, and 9 o'clock.

DERRING'S PATENT LIGHT SUMMER

the Bank via the Angel, Islington and the City Road. It not only carried the heaviest traffic from the growing north-western suburbs but also ran round the northern fringes of the metropolis. It therefore lay outside the Hackney coach monopoly zone and vehicles could stop at will to pick up or set down their passengers. The route also offered plenty of middle class traffic, especially from the Paddington and Marylebone end.

Shillibeer placed great emphasis on speed, punctuality and what we would now call customer care: 'The other coaches,' he commented, 'hang about at the public houses a quarter of an hour or ten minutes, but I go right away whether I have passengers or not.' Although an hour was allowed, it was then apparently possible to do the journey of 5 miles in 40 minutes. Today, when the Marylebone, Euston and City roads are often jammed, this is the edge of the Congestion Zone and a modern bus journey would be no faster.

Shillibeer's omnibus was well supported by the public from the start. *The Times* reported at the end of the first week's service that 'fourteen or fifteen ladies and gentlemen were frequently to be seen running after it when it was completely full'. Inevitably, it aroused fierce opposition from the short stage drivers, but Shillibeer's success soon prompted many imitators. Other operators began running omnibus services all over London, particularly once public pressure had led to the lifting of the Hackney carriage monopoly in 1832.

Did you know?

George Shillibeer (1797–1866) was certainly an innovator but a poor businessman who seemed unable to manage his finances. In the face of increasing competition, and persistent problems with dishonest employees who defrauded him of his takings, he went bankrupt in 1831. Unable to pay his debts, he was sent to debtors' prison. On his release, he quickly set up another omnibus service in south London, but got into debt again and spent a second term in debtors' prison. He then gave up on buses and went into the undertaking business, devising a patent funeral carriage which he later displayed at the Great Exhibition in 1851.

When he died in 1866 Shillibeer was a forgotten figure and his name only became familiar again when the centenary of the first London bus service was celebrated in 1929. The London General Omnibus Company built a replica of his original omnibus, which is now on display in the London Transport Museum.

A portrait of Shillibeer in later years aged about sixty.

3
Horse Bus London

New services sprang up, with rival omnibus operators competing for passengers, often racing each other to pick up fares. There were no fixed stops and passengers could in theory hail an omnibus anywhere on either side of the road, hoping the driver would respond. To stop the vehicle once on board, passengers would bang on the roof or pull on a cord inside the bus which was attached to the driver's arm. It was all pretty hit and miss, and omnibus crews soon had an unsavoury reputation as cads and hustlers even though they were licensed.

Did you know?

Charles Dickens was one of the first journalists to satirise the colourful experience of London bus travel in his 'Street Sketches' for the *Morning Chronicle* in 1834. 'We are not aware,' he writes, 'that it has ever been precisely ascertained how

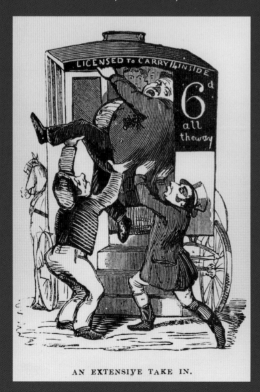

AN EXTENSIVE TAKE IN.

many passengers our omnibus will contain. The impression on the cad's mind evidently is that it is amply sufficient for the accommodation of any number of persons that can be enticed into it. "Any room?" cries a hot pedestrian. "Plenty o' room, sir," replies the conductor, gradually opening the door, and not disclosing the real state of the case, until the wretched man is on the steps. "Where?" enquires the entrapped individual, with an attempt to back out again. "Either side, sir" rejoins the cad, shoving him in and slamming the door. "All right, Bill." Retreat is impossible; the new comer rolls about, till he falls down somewhere and there he stops.'

'An Extensive Take In'. This contemporary cartoon fits Dickens' description in the *Morning Chronicle*, 1834.

By the mid-1830s there were nearly 400 licensed horse buses in London. All of them were two-horse vehicles, easier to handle than Shillibeer's three-horse coach on the narrow, crowded streets of the built-up central area. Omnibuses were also gradually ousting the old short stagecoaches from routes running out of town. As competition grew in the 1840s, operators introduced vehicles with lighter frames and a raised roof, which allowed space for rather precarious outside seating. These omnibuses were soon known as Knife-boards because of the shape of the bench seat along the top of the roof, which resembled the domestic knife-cleaning boards used in Victorian kitchens.

Access to the roof was by climbing metal rungs on both sides of the door at the back, which effectively made the top deck a men-only preserve in the age of the crinoline. The rungs were later replaced from the 1860s by a curved staircase from a platform, which made access easier for all, and 'decency boards' were fitted to the top decks which were used for advertising. These were the original double-deckers, and the basic hardy design of the standard London horse bus, which could seat about twenty-six passengers inside and out, remained almost unchanged throughout the nineteenth century. The knifeboard seat on top was replaced on new buses by two rows of forward-facing garden seats from the 1880s, but there were no significant further improvements in vehicle layout or construction.

As the numbers and the competition grew, so 'associations' of owners who worked certain routes in common emerged. On a particular route the various proprietors, while maintaining their individual ownership of a vehicle, organised the service jointly, and allocated 'times' in which each operator ran his bus. All the buses on a route were then painted the same colour and carried the name of the association. Receipts were pooled and paid out in proportion to the number of buses worked by each proprietor.

A Favorite horse bus at Islington Green, painted by James Pollard, 1852. The Favorite fleet, run by E & J Wilson of Holloway, was one of the largest in London. It was later taken over by the LGOC.

The Great Exhibition of 1851 was one of London's first major visitor attractions. 6 million day trippers and tourists flocked to the Crystal Palace in Hyde Park to see it. It created a boom in the bus business, but brought only short-term profits. Bus operators were soon faced with a slump when the great show ended and there were too many buses on the streets looking for passengers.

The crisis was resolved by the creation of a single giant bus company for London, a process which followed a major reorganisation and amalgamation of bus services in Paris. The Compagnie Generale des Omnibus de Londres began life in 1855 as an Anglo-French enterprise with offices in both capitals. Like Shillibeer, its creators were originally inspired by French practice, but the name and operation was quickly anglicised to become the London General Omnibus Company (LGOC) in 1856.

Within a few months the General had acquired ownership of 600 of London's 810 omnibuses. Only a few well-run family operations, such as Tilling and Birch, stayed independent, while the LGOC had suddenly become the largest bus company in the world, attempting to establish a consistent level of service across the metropolis. The LGOC's records show that in its first year, the average number of buses running each day was 450. To provide the service the General maintained nearly 6,000 horses, each one covering

Above: The boom before the bust. Tourists and trippers hurrying to the Crystal Palace exhibition. A cartoon by George Cruikshank, 1851. **Left**: Bankers and clerks arriving for work in the City at 9 a.m. An illustration from *Twice Round the Clock in London* by George Augustus Sala, 1861.

12 miles a day in harness. The animals each consumed 16 pounds of bruised oats and 10 pounds of hay and straw mixture every day.

The LGOC never achieved a monopoly of horse bus operations in London, but it quickly came to dominate the market. With the removal of most remaining tolls and taxes, the General was able to make fairly good profits throughout the second half of the century. Although there was competition on some routes from the new tramways and underground railways, the number of omnibus passengers continued to rise steadily. In 1885 the LGOC carried nearly 77 million passengers; by 1890 this figure had risen to over 112 million.

When permanent street tramways were opened in London from 1870 onwards, they catered for a different market. By using larger vehicles with twice the capacity of an omnibus, tramway companies could afford to offer lower fares. A pair of horses could manage a much larger and heavier vehicle running on rails because there was less rolling resistance.

Like the railways from the 1860s, the tram companies were obliged by law to provide special workmen's tickets, usually at half price, in the early morning and after 6 p.m. The first tram on the North Metropolitan system was at 4.45 a.m. Omnibuses, by contrast, did not start running before 8 a.m., far too late for working class travellers to get to their place of work, but well timed for City clerks.

The last quarter of the nineteenth century saw an almost continuous increase in traffic on both omnibuses and trams. In the mid-1870s, the LGOC, its 200 associates and a handful of independent omnibus operators were carrying 49 million passengers a year, while the three tramway companies carried about the same. Twenty years later both had nearly quadrupled their traffic, to about 300 million and 280 million passengers respectively.

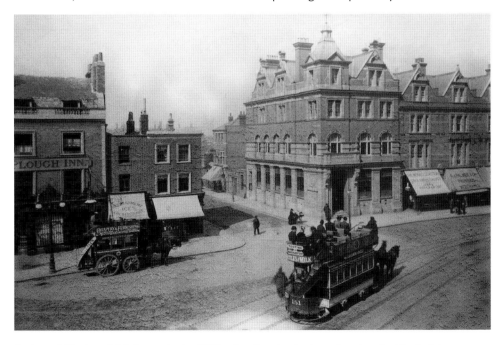

A view of Clapham High Street in the 1880s, showing clearly that a London double-deck horse tram (right) was twice the size and capacity of a bus (left).

Above: A horse bus about to climb Rosslyn Hill to Hampstead Village, with a trace horse attached at the front to assist on the ascent, 1887.
Left: Veteran LGOC horse bus driver William Parragreen, known as 'cast iron Billy', with his conductor in 1877.

The London omnibus operators soon dropped their opposition to tramways and quietly came to agreements with them that suited both parties, almost making them partners rather than rivals. The LGOC even became the main supplier of horses to the North Metropolitan Tramways and there were soon shared stabling arrangements between the companies. They also agreed to service changes so that buses and trams were not in direct competition on the same streets. Tramlines appeared along most of London's inner suburban main roads, but opposition and hostility remained when trams tried to penetrate the busy central areas of the City and West End. These districts would remain tram-free and dominated by buses into the twentieth century.

Did you know?

The social contrast between buses and trams was pointed out in a patronising article in the *Cornhill Magazine* in 1890. London omnibuses, the writer observed, were becoming more comfortable and convenient to use and as a result, 'ladies and gentlemen, officers, members of first class clubs even, all patronise the once despised "bus"'. At the same time, 'the working man is rarely seen on the upholstered cushions; he feels himself uncomfortable and de trop. The tramcar is his familiar vehicle and he can ensconce himself there in his mortar-splashed clothes without restraint'.

After just six years' operation the London tramways were carrying almost as many passengers as the LGOC buses, with each travel mode recording just under 50 million passengers in 1875. These numbers trebled on both buses and trams over the next twenty-five years. Clearly the overall market for urban transport was growing as London's population grew and the city expanded, but taking the bus remained an essentially middle class experience in the Victorian metropolis.

By the 1890s London horse buses were carrying well over 150 million passengers a year in a city that was home to around 4 million people. Just over 2,100 buses were running on 176 routes, requiring around 25,000 horses. But an ever-expanding market could not disguise the looming financial, logistical and environmental problems caused by London's absolute reliance and dependence on the horse.

Operating horse buses was an expensive business, as the horses needed far more care and attention than the hardy wooden vehicles they pulled. The main companies built and maintained their own vehicles, in the LGOC's case mostly using their large coachworks in Islington. There were also several large stables across London, some of them shared by the bus and tram companies.

It made financial sense to look after the animals well. The horses were the most costly of a bus company's assets, while most of the unskilled men were dispensable and easily replaced. Bus crews were poorly paid, and had no job security. There was always a large turnover of labour on Victorian horse buses and trams, especially in London.

Horses, on the other hand, were chosen carefully and generally well cared for. Their working life on the buses was short and tough, on average a maximum of five years (four on the trams). Each bus required twelve horses, working in pairs, to stay on the road, with extra trace horses needed to assist on hilly routes. The cost of stabling, feed and vets' fees

London horse bus stables in Hackney, c. 1890.

The road junction at the Bank (right) and Mansion House (left) in the morning rush hour c. 1900. The clock on the Mappin & Webb building in the centre reads 8.40 a.m.

was considerable. There were also unpredictable risks such as a sharp rise in the cost of feed following a poor harvest, or an outbreak of serious disease in the stables such as equine influenza or 'pinkeye'. On top of these issues, the sheer quantity of horse manure dumped on the streets every day was a growing health and environmental problem, although few people seemed to recognise this at the time. The horse was outgrowing the city and a suitable replacement was needed.

Above: Horse buses at Hyde Park Corner, 1903. ***Right***: A horse bus conductor, *c.* 1900. Bell Punch ticket machines like the one he is wearing were used by the LGOC from the 1890s. His bus shows the chaotic mixture of travel information and advertising on all London buses at this time.

4

The Motor Bus Revolution: 1900-1914

At the dawn of the twentieth century, road transport in London was still entirely dependent on horse power. Steam passenger railways had been operating in the metropolis since 1836, with the opening of the world's first underground railway, the Metropolitan, in 1863. The first deep-level electric tube had opened in 1890 and two more were operating by 1900.

Mechanisation on the roads was much slower. Mechanically powered road vehicles, in the form of steam carriages devised by Walter Hancock, began services in London as early as the 1830s, but none of them survived for long or were reliable enough to provide a regular public service. Road safety concerns by the licensing authorities and slowness in developing a suitable power source delayed the arrival of the motor bus until the Edwardian era.

Electric power had been successfully applied to tramways in a number of American and European cities in the 1890s, though the first London line, in the western suburbs, was not opened until 1901. London's first motor bus service, using two experimental vehicles with German Daimler petrol engines, lasted only a few months from October 1899 to December 1900. Alternatives to the internal combustion engine, including battery electric, petrol-electric and steam buses (fired with paraffin) were all tried out on the streets of London. Tilling's fleet of petrol-electrics and Clarkson's National steam buses had some years of operational success but neither vehicle had the potential to replace the horse.

The LGOC, like other bus undertakings, had for some years appreciated that it had to find an acceptable form of mechanical traction. The challenge of the electric tube railway, coupled with various imminent schemes for electrifying London's tramways and the high cost of horse fodder, gave a sharp impetus to the quest.

Breaking up horse buses in the LGOC yard at Holloway, 1911.

Above: Steam coaches and carriages were first devised by Walter Hancock in the early 1830s. They worked, but not well enough to provide a reliable and sustainable public service.
Below: The new and the old at Charing Cross, February 1900. This was the first 'regular' motor bus service in London using what was essentially a horse bus fitted with a 4-cylinder German Daimler engine.

A London Motor Omnibus Co. Milnes-Daimler being prepared for the first long-distance run to Brighton, 1905.

Clarkson paraffin-fired steam bus at Nunhead garage, 1912.

The first attempt by the LGOC to experiment with a motor bus involved importing a Fischer petrol-electric chassis from the USA, which arrived in 1903. A petrol engine was employed to drive a dynamo. The current was stored in accumulators and the wheels were then driven by motors powered by the battery. The LGOC fitted it with a double-deck body, but on trial the petrol consumption was so great and the tyre wear so heavy that the bus was never put into service and was returned to its makers. The General's first toe in the water of mechanisation was not encouraging.

In 1905 the first boom in motor bus operation took place, with a series of small independent companies entering the field. The twenty motor buses of various types operating on London's streets in January 1905 grew to more than 200 by the end of the year, but nearly all these pioneer enterprises failed. Numbers increased rapidly again in 1906–7, but the industry was in an uncertain period of flux, with rapid but inconsistent technological change and development. Most experimental developments by small companies fell by the wayside, and although the main horse bus companies stopped building their traditional vehicles, they were also wary about investing too heavily and quickly in a mechanised future. The caution and conservatism of the LGOC, still the major horse bus operator, worked to its advantage as smaller rivals over-invested in unproven motor vehicles and went to the wall.

Having bided its time, in 1908 the LGOC made successful takeover bids for two of its leading rivals in motor bus operation, the London Road Car Company (fleet name Union Jack) and the London Motor Omnibus Company (fleet name Vanguard). After the merger, the enlarged General owned 885 of the 1,066 motor buses then operating in London, many of which ran on imported European engines and chassis like Büssing (German), and de Dion Bouton (French). Some were based on Anglo-European partnerships such as Milnes-Daimler, whose vehicles had German Daimler engines and bodywork by the British tram builders Milnes.

These vehicles were now all in single ownership, but maintenance and operation of such a mixed fleet across the capital was difficult and somewhat haphazard. Very few of these early motor buses turned out to be either hardy or reliable. As a result, the LGOC decided to use the new motor works at Walthamstow that it inherited from Vanguard as a central development and production facility to shape its own future.

The combined expertise and experience of the merged 'big three' was pooled to develop and build a standard motor bus for London. A new vehicle emerged in 1909 known as the X-type, the LGOC's first motor bus design and production of its own. Within a year it was adapted and refined to become the remarkable B-type, launched in October 1910. It looked primitive, with its wooden open-top body almost unchanged from the horse bus, but the B-type was rugged, reliable and cheap to run. This bus would invalidate the unwise but much quoted prophecy made a year earlier by A. L. C. Fell, chief officer of the London County Council Tramways, that 'twenty years hence motor buses will be exhibited as curios in museums'.

The B-type was designed by Frank Searle, the LGOC's chief motor engineer, and his assistant Walter James Iden, works manager at Walthamstow. Searle cheerfully acknowledged having 'cribbed shamelessly' in its development. As he said of the X-type, its immediate predecessor, 'any parts of the 28 types which had stood up to the gruelling of the London streets were embodied in it'. Hybrid it may have been, but the B-type was a winning combination of parts.

The LGOC soon equipped Walthamstow for full mass production of the new bus. Nearly 3,000 B-type engine units and chassis were turned out here by 1914. The B-type was

The LGOC's X-type, 'cribbed shamelessly' from the various bus types operating in 1909.

effectively the bus equivalent of Henry Ford's Model T automobile, which first appeared in the USA in 1908 and was being assembled on production lines in Detroit and Trafford Park, Manchester, by 1913. The B-type was the first commercial vehicle developed in the UK to be built in the same way.

The B-type was so successful and reliable that the LGOC was able to confidently replace every horse bus in its fleet by 1911. In that same year, Searle was poached by the Daimler company to design a rival to the B-type that the company could sell to independent operators. Meanwhile, the Walthamstow bus works was floated as a separately quoted company on the London Stock Exchange, known as the Associated Equipment Company (AEC).

This was a fast-moving period of rapid merger and amalgamation on the buses. AEC was controlled by the LGOC, and from 1912 the General itself became part of the Underground Group, often known at the time as the London Traffic Combine, as the organisation now dominated much of the bus, tram and underground railway operation in the capital. Outside it were the tramway operations of the London County Council, various smaller council tram operators in east and south-east London, and the Metropolitan Railway.

AEC became the principal builder of London's buses for the next six decades, first for the LGOC and, after 1933, for London Transport. The partnership was to continue until the production of the Routemaster in the 1960s. AEC was then taken over by Leyland Motors and eventually closed down in the 1970s.

The rapid move to modern mass production methods could not immediately be matched on the wooden body building side, which was initially carried out in traditional craft style at the LGOC's three London coachworks. Despite mechanisation, the overall layout and design

Above: An early output of B type chassis with engines at the Walthamstow works, 1910. These will have bodies fitted at one of the LGOC's former horse bus coachworks.
Below: B-type buses on their first day of service at the LGOC's Cricklewood garage, 1911.

of motor buses still reflected that of their horse-drawn predecessors at this stage. Industrial innovation could provide some solutions but it was constrained in London by Metropolitan Police regulations, which reflected a cautious official approach to vehicle weight and size based on fears of traffic accidents and damage to road surfaces from heavy motor vehicles.

As a result, the B-type was limited to an un-laden weight of 3.5 tons, a capacity of thirty-four passengers and a top speed of 12 mph. However, such was its success that within two years of its introduction the AEC factory was employing 1,700 men, who were building bus engines and chassis at a rate of up to thirty a week. The wooden bodies were still built and fitted in the LGOC's coachworks in Islington by the same men who had built the horse buses.

Did you know?

Walter James Iden, the works manager at AEC, was responsible for setting up what amounted to Britain's first motor bus factory at Walthamstow, where the B-types were constructed. Recalling the process in 1926 when the last B-type was withdrawn, Iden wrote that: 'The finest and most up-to-date plant was installed for their construction at Walthamstow and here were established nearly every branch necessary for complete manufacture, including foundries for aluminium and yellow metal, tinsmiths, pattern, machine shops etc. The only items purchased outside were such things as steel castings, stampings and most of the finished crankshafts; but every engine unit and chassis was erected on the premises.'

Liberated by a dependable fleet of motor buses, routes expanded beyond the traditional built-up area of London to serve districts and new suburbs springing up in the Home Counties. Horse buses were limited by the physical capacity of the horses, but motor buses could travel further and faster, even with a 12 mph speed limit.

Free bus maps issued by the LGOC from 1911 showed the rapid growth: from twenty-three on the first map to more than 100 by spring 1914. Routes were now clearly numbered on each vehicle and the LGOC decided to use a standard bright red colour scheme to distinguish its fleet from the buses of other operators in London. LGOC bus crews were issued with a smart company uniform for the first time, their brass cap badges featuring the newly devised company logo, a winged wheel.

The General also quickly became adept at publicity as operations grew. Their printed maps, issued at least twice a year, carried well-chosen slogans that promoted the motor bus over the Underground and trams: 'Open Air to Everywhere', 'Travel above Ground' and even a dubiously attributed quote from Gladstone that 'the best way to see London is from the top of a bus.'

When the UERL took over the LGOC in 1912, coordination of the different transport modes in the London Traffic Combine replaced the previous atmosphere of competition in the company's publicity. Albert Stanley, later Lord Ashfield, who had become the UERL's managing director in 1910, had engineered the merger and put Frank Pick in charge of the Combine's traffic promotion and development. At a time when the Underground Group was struggling with debt and too few passengers on the new Tubes, the acquisition of the main

Above: An early motor bus route map published by the LGOC, 1911.
Below: LGOC B-type buses at Mortlake garage, west London, *c.* 1912. The staff are smartly dressed in their new uniforms, with the drivers wearing their summer dustcoats.

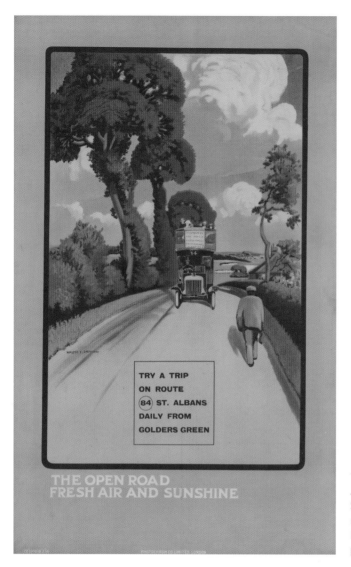

TRY A TRIP
ON ROUTE
(84) ST. ALBANS
DAILY FROM
GOLDERS GREEN

THE OPEN ROAD
FRESH AIR AND SUNSHINE

'The Open Road', 1914. A poster by Walter Spradbery, one of the artists regularly commissioned by Frank Pick in his successful poster programme.

bus company was an astute business opportunity. Twenty years later, the dynamic duo of Ashfield and Pick would be running London Transport.

As commercial manager for the combined operation from 1912, Pick promoted the buses and Underground as integrated and coordinated services. Feeder bus routes extended the reach of the Underground for commuters in the suburbs and new Sunday bus services from outer stations took day trippers as far from London as Windsor Castle in the west and St. Albans in the north. Pick was already getting a reputation for his high quality poster publicity and new commissions promoted leisure use of both bus, tram and Underground services with encouraging traffic results. He and Stanley both recognised that it was the integration and coordination of London's transport services that was key, rather than competition between them. A reliable, mechanised bus service was an essential contributor to the whole.

5
The First World War: 1914–1918

At the outbreak of the First World War in August 1914, there was a general expectation in Britain that it would be 'all over by Christmas'. The conflict was to drag on for over four years and have an enormous effect on society, with shocking casualties and unprecedented social and economic changes far beyond the battlefields.

An almost immediate practical impact was felt on London's buses. With insufficient motor vehicles of its own to sustain a war in Europe, the British Army had to requisition over a thousand London buses (about one third of the capital's fleet). These were sent to France, accompanied by their drivers, who were recruited into the Army Service Corps (ASC). A touch of London was brought to the Western Front as convoys of buses, initially with their bright red livery, adverts and route boards intact, carried troops into the front line and brought the wounded out.

British Tommies transported by bus to the front line in Flanders, 1914. Khaki now replaced red.

A B-type serving as a pigeon loft on the Western Front, 1916.

The sturdy B-type chassis was equally suitable for lorry work and over 8,000 were built by AEC at Walthamstow for this purpose. Six of the buses were even converted into mobile military pigeon lofts on the Western Front. Homing pigeons were a reliable means of communication, released from battle areas to their home lofts behind the lines carrying messages for HQ.

Did you know?

Stories of the buses' activities on the Western Front appeared regularly in the LGOC's staff magazine, including a photograph of one that had to be abandoned at St Eloi when it was caught in crossfire after carrying forward troops from the London Scottish Regiment to a disastrous charge. The driver's snapshot of the badly damaged bus left in no-man's land was later widely used for publicity by AEC with the caption, 'Born at Walthamstow. Died in France.'

Including the large number of reservists and volunteer drivers who joined up in August 1914, over 10,000 LGOC staff served in various capacities in the forces. 810 of them were killed on active service. As more and more men joined up, the LGOC began, somewhat reluctantly, to recruit women 'substitutes' to maintain the severely reduced skeleton bus service in wartime London.

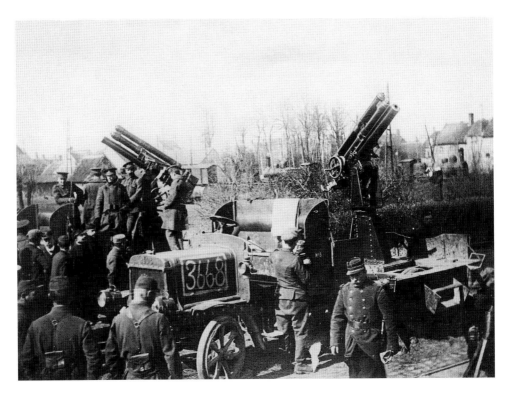

Above: The robust B-type bus and lorry chassis were very versatile. Anti-aircraft guns were mounted onto bus chassis at the front line to provide mobile artillery.

Right: Florence Cordell, who became an LGOC conductor at Willesden garage in 1916, photographed in her new uniform. This included leather lace-up gaiters worn over boots which came up to the knee.

The first poster to recruit female conductors in March 1916 attracted 20,000 applicants. To qualify, the women had to be taller than five feet and aged between twenty-one and thirty-five. Nearly half of those taken on as conductors had previously been employed as domestic servants. As conductors, they were doing a more interesting job, were better paid and had fixed working hours.

Over the next three years, the LGOC employed some 3,500 women both as uniformed conductors and in behind the scenes roles at bus garages as cleaners, painters and mechanics. All of them were doing jobs never previously open to women, and the 'conductorettes' in particular were the most visible new female employment role, which arose on the Home Front. Nearly all of them had to give up their new jobs in 1919 as the men returned, and bus work was not available to women again until the Second World War broke out twenty years later.

Did you know?

The driver and conductor of a B-type were both killed when their bus on route 8 was hit in a Zeppelin raid on London in 1915. Their funeral in the East End was a major public event, with the cortege led through Dalston by wreathed B-type buses and a large contingent of their colleagues wearing white summer dustcoats. The badly damaged bus on which they died, B804, was repaired and put back into service.

B43, one of the survivors of the Western Front, visited Buckingham Palace in 1920, when the bus and twenty-five veteran busmen were presented to King George V. The King remarked that this was the first time he had stepped on a bus, and invited the men and their bus to join the Remembrance parade being planned around the new Whitehall Cenotaph in November on Armistice Day. The bus

FUNERAL OF VICTIMS OF AIR RAID. DRIVER TARRANT AND CONDUCTOR ROGERS. L.G.O.C. 20/10/15. E.S. 2.

and veteran drivers then took part in the London Remembrance Parade annually. Transport for London staff continue this tradition today. B43 is now on static display in the Imperial War Museum.

Opposite: The funeral of driver Tarrant and conductor Rogers, both killed in a Zeppelin raid on east London in October 1915.
Right: Their badly damaged bus was repaired and put back into service. .

6

Progress and Pirates: The 1920s

The forty-six-seat K–type, carrying twelve more passengers than the B-type, was introduced in August 1919, only nine months after the Armistice. There was a desperate shortage of buses at this time, which meant lorries had to be used temporarily on some routes. Police regulations revised in 1917, together with the introduction of the eight-hour day, which increased labour costs, made the introduction of larger capacity vehicles essential. The driver was now placed beside the engine instead of behind it, which lengthened the space available for passengers.

The longer S-type, introduced in 1920, raised the seating capacity further to fifty-four passengers and forced the authorities to increase the weight limit to 8.5 tons. It was clear that as larger buses were developed, there would be regular conflict with the Metropolitan Police over the permissible length, width and weight of vehicles. This also applied to other improvements such as covered tops and enclosed cabs as well as pneumatic tyres, all accepted by the late 1920s after lengthy battles with the licensing authority over safety.

Did you know?

In 1921 the LGOC opened a large new works at Chiswick in west London. Its purpose was to centralise the repair, overhaul and construction of buses. It was set up by George Shave, the chief engineer, using the flowline system developed by Ford and other car makers in Detroit, USA. Every vehicle in the LGOC fleet was sent to Chiswick once a year to be completely stripped down and virtually rebuilt, with the body and chassis moving

continually on a production line. Each bus was then reassembled and rigorously tested before going back into service. By the 1930s the total staff at the works had grown to about 3,000 and Chiswick included a training school for drivers and conductors.

The 'flow line' overhaul system used at Chiswick Works from 1926. The S-type chassis frames are attached to a moving assembly line below the floor.

During the 1920s buses began to resemble modern vehicles. It was a decade of particularly dramatic design and engineering development, aided by the gradual relaxation of the licensing regulations. Seating capacity increased as the size of vehicles grew, enclosed top decks were eventually permitted, pneumatic tyres replaced solid rubber, roller blinds superseded wooden destination boards and comfortable cushion seating covered in woollen moquette became a standard feature of London buses.

Many of the improvements were stimulated by competition between the LGOC and a rash of new independent bus operators, dismissively branded as 'pirates' by the General. The independents were mostly supplied by rival manufacturers to AEC such

An Underground Group poster of 1920 promising improvements to the problems of overcrowding in London. The new buses at the bottom are the LGOC's K-types, just being introduced.

The bonnet and driver's cab of the K-type, positioned beside the engine rather than behind it, as on the B-type. This is London Transport Museum's K424, still in full operating condition aged 100. (Author)

The first of the pirates. Arthur Partridge set up his independent Chocolate Express company in 1922 using Leyland LB buses. This example was restored to working order by Mike Sutcliffe and is now in the London Transport Museum collection. (Mike Sutcliffe)

as Dennis and Leyland. More than 250 'pirate' operators flourished across London from 1922, but the London Traffic Act of 1924 regulated the number of buses allowed on the streets. Despite some public sympathy for the independent operators, they had little chance of succeeding against the growing power of the General. Bus builders other than AEC were equally keen to use the independents as a way into the London bus market that AEC dominated. It was Leyland's chief engineer, George John Rackham, who designed the Titan in 1927. This was a real breakthrough in bus design and a considerable improvement on the latest AEC/LGOC vehicle, the NS-type of 1923. The Titan boasted a six-cylinder overhead camshaft engine to the NS-type's four-cylinder side-valve unit.

The NS had been designed with a cranked 'drop' chassis which had a very low centre of gravity. This meant that it could safely accommodate a top cover without the risk of tilting, or so the LGOC hoped. At this stage the Metropolitan Police was not convinced and at least 1,700 open-top NS-types had been built over a two-year period before the first covered double-deckers were licensed for service. Rackham's more sophisticated Titan made its first appearance at about the same time, but initially was only bought by independent operators in London. It too had a chassis layout which enabled a low-slung body to be fitted, and this in turn was designed to take lightweight aluminium panelling throughout.

Right: 'Summer Outings' poster by
L. B. Black, 1926. The bus is an S-type.
Below: Buses at Marble Arch, 1930,
showing the rapid progress in design
from the open-top, solid-tyred K-type
(centre, 1919) via an NS-type with a
covered top (left, 1925) to a fully enclosed
ST-type of 1929 (right).

The Leyland Titan was in many respects the first truly modern bus. Within a year of its appearance, Rackham had been headhunted by AEC to become its chief engineer. AEC was then in the process of moving from Walthamstow to a new factory in west London at Southall, and wanted to offer the LGOC a bus that could better the Titans being snapped up by provincial operators and the remaining London independents. The result was the AEC Regal single-decker, Regent four-wheel double-decker and Renown six-wheel double-decker. Production models of all three, classified by the LGOC as T, ST and LT-types, were on the streets of London by 1930, and became the mainstay of the General's fleet.

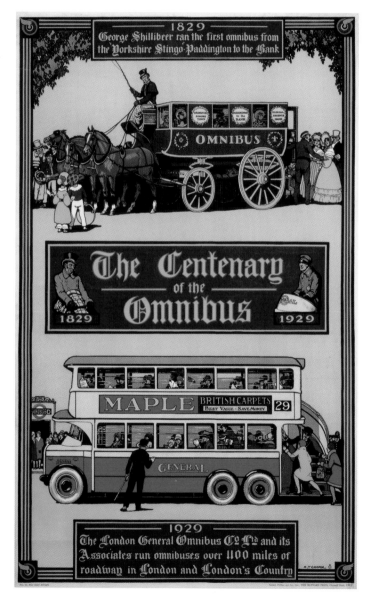

Poster celebrating the centenary of the London bus, 1929. The LGOC built a working replica of Shillibeer's original three-horse omnibus and introduced its latest motor vehicle to the streets, the six-wheeled LT-type.

7

Towards London Transport: The 1930s

By the early 1930s the bus had become London's most popular form of public transport. Passenger journeys by road and rail in Greater London increased by 30 per cent in the 1920s, but this overall travel figure hid striking variations between modes. Underground and local railway traffic grew steadily and use of the trams remained constant but bus travel boomed. The total number of bus journeys made had more than doubled in a decade. Even the process of catching the bus had become more formal, with the progressive introduction of bus stops from 1921 and the creation of complete bus stations at busy termini such as Victoria.

The LGOC, working with its main supplier AEC, continued to make rapid progress in vehicle development and engineering at Chiswick. New buses were increasingly reliable, easier to maintain and, most importantly, attractive and comfortable for passengers. The STL-type, launched in 1932, which became the standard London double-decker of the period, was a huge advance on the open-top, solid-tyred buses of ten years earlier.

Motor buses were cheaper to run than trams and far more flexible. Unlike trams, they did not require any fixed infrastructure and can be steered round obstacles in the street. The bus network continued to expand but at this stage it complemented the heavily used tram system rather than offering an alternative to it. Motor buses were still not large enough to supersede trams on a one-for-one basis.

In 1931 the first electric trolleybuses replaced trams on some suburban routes in south-west London. A trolleybus is a cross between a tram and a bus, electrically powered through overhead wires but not confined to rails in the road. Successful operating experience

Poster encouraging hikers to get out into London's country on the new Green Line coach services, by Frances Halsted, 1932.

Above and left: An STL-type double-decker at a bus stop in Hanwell, 1939. London Transport had recently extended the bus stop system right across London, using the clear new flags for compulsory and request stops designed by 'Zero' (Hans Schleger).

with this hybrid system soon led to trolleybuses rather than motor buses being selected for the wholesale replacement of London's huge tram network.

The most significant spur to progress on the streets in the 1930s was the creation of London Transport. After years of debate but little action, a single public transport authority was established by the government in July 1933. The London Passenger Transport Board (LPTB) became responsible for running all bus, tram and underground railway services over a vast urban and country area across and around Greater London.

At a time when very few people owned a car, the LPTB had to plan for the transport needs of more than 9 million residents. Lord Ashfield became its first chairman and Frank Pick the vice chairman and chief executive, bringing his eagle eye for good design to an even wider range of transport infrastructure and vehicles. Buses were arguably the most important and versatile part of London Transport's operations, and the only section of the organisation that was profitable, effectively cross-subsidising essential tram and Underground services.

With the creation of London Transport, it was the end of the road for the remaining independents. Their vehicles, which had introduced many new features in bus design, were compulsorily purchased and absorbed with all the LGOC's buses into the LPTB fleet. There would be little room for independent bus operation on the streets of London for the next fifty years.

After 1933 London Transport followed the LGOC's policy of standardising its bus fleet as far as possible. Double-deckers remained the standard high-capacity London vehicles with some single-deckers for hilly or lightly used suburban and country routes. Single-deck coaches were also required for excursion services and for use on the new Green Line routes introduced from 1930 onwards, which provided express services across central London and out to towns in London's countryside.

A size comparison in Chiswick High Road, 1937. From left to right: a T-type Green Line coach (thirty seats), an STL-type double-decker (fifty-six seats) and a standard trolleybus (seventy seats).

A panel poster by Tom Eckersley and Eric Lombers, 1935. New cinemas opened in every London suburb in the 1930s and going out to the 'pictures' became everyone's favourite entertainment.

A Green Line coach leaves the new LPTB stop and shelter in Stevenage High Street on its way to Baldock, the northern limit of the huge new London Transport country area, 1934.

Did you know?

At its very first meeting in July 1933, the new board took the important decision to use oil (diesel) engines in all its buses, on the basis that this would save some £120 a year in the running costs of each vehicle. With this move, which followed extensive experimental trials by the LGOC, London Transport set a national trend. All subsequent new orders were for diesel buses, although because of the war, conversion of the existing petrol-engined fleet was not completed until 1950.

The standard London Transport bus of the 1930s was the STL-type, which used a lengthened version of the AEC Regent chassis. Its body layout, essentially a fully enclosed box except for the half cab and open rear platform, remained the archetypal form of the London Transport double-decker bus until the 1960s. Other British towns favoured broadly similar, though often less robust, designs while many Continental cities like Paris went over entirely to single-deck bus operation. The London bus was beginning to stand out as a distinct and recognisably different vehicle, the product of a unique engineering and design culture that was specific to the partnership between LT at Chiswick and AEC at Southall.

A wet night in Regent Street at Piccadilly Circus, 1935, with at least a dozen buses crowding the street and practically no other traffic. With no trams or trolleybuses allowed, the West End was virtually dominated by buses at this time.

A streamlined
TF-type Green
Line coach, built
on a Leyland Tiger
chassis, 1939.
One of many
advanced London
Transport designs
from Chiswick
in the 1930s, in
this case with an
underfloor engine.
(John F. Stiles)

Many of the experiments in bus design tried out in London in this period now seem to have been ahead of their time and some were only taken up many years later. The AEC Q-type of 1932, for example, had a side-mounted engine, which allowed a front-entrance double-deck body to be fitted. It looks very similar to the design style adopted almost universally for British double-deckers since the 1960s but it was not adopted by London Transport in the 1930s. Later trials with an underfloor engine gave even more scope for changing the body design and layout. This was first tried out in 1939 with the elegant TF-type Green Line coach, built on a Leyland Tiger chassis, which foreshadowed many post-war developments.

For the majority of its fleet, London Transport followed an evolutionary rather than a revolutionary design development process. This was certainly true of the classic RT (Regent Three) type, which was eventually mass produced after the war in greater quantity than any other bus. When the prototype appeared in 1939 it did not look very different to the STL, but in every detail its design conformed to the high quality, practical and, by this stage, rather refined and elegant Chiswick approach.

For Londoners and residents of the Home Counties this must have seemed like a golden age on the buses. A growing fleet of modern, bright red vehicles criss-crossed central London and the suburbs, with green buses and coaches running far out into London's country. From 1934 all of them carried the name London Transport in gold Johnston Underground lettering. This also appeared with the distinctive bar and circle symbol on new bus stops and shelters across London and far into the surrounding countryside. The LPTB territory covered 2,000 square miles within a 30-mile radius of Charing Cross. It stretched north to Baldock, west to High Wycombe, south to Horsham and east to Gravesend. Staff and services were smart and efficient, and the very reasonable penny a mile fares never went up. It couldn't last.

Just before the Coronation in 1937, London Transport busmen went on strike for better wages and conditions. Two years later, when the LPTB was about to increase bus fares for the first time as costs escalated, a much more serious event intervened. From 3 September 1939 Britain was at war with Germany again and London's bus services took on new roles in the national emergency.

8

War and Austerity: The 1940s

There had been no civilian preparations for war in 1914. Twenty-five years later, the radio announcement to the nation on 3 September 1939 by the Prime Minister that 'this country is at war with Germany' came as no great surprise. For more than a year Hitler's aggressive stance towards Nazi Germany's European neighbours had threatened to plunge the Continent into chaos.

By September 1938, when the Munich crisis arose, London Transport had prepared detailed defence plans, which would allow it to remain operational should the capital come under aerial bombardment – the greatest fear of the time.

On 1 September 1939, two days before the official declaration of war, plans for the mass evacuation of the city were put in place. Over four days nearly half a million people, mainly children and expectant mothers, were conveyed out of London by bus and train. Hospital patients were removed by Green Line coaches swiftly converted into temporary ambulances. Many bus drivers had no sleep for 48 hours.

Blackout restrictions were applied immediately and London Transport's petrol and oil supplies were cut by 25 per cent as an economy measure. Bus services were reduced or withdrawn altogether to save fuel and within four months more than 800 red buses were lying idle.

The London Blitz began with a mass bombing raid on 7 September 1940, after which the city was bombed heavily every night until 2 November. Attacks then continued intermittently until May 1941. In fifty-seven raids on the city more than 15,000 civilians were killed and many more made homeless.

The damage and disruption to the London Transport system was severe but never crippling. A service of some kind could nearly always be maintained, though this was more

London Transport Museum's LT-type dressed for war, with headlamp cowls and windows netted to protect against splintering in a bomb blast. This bus can now be seen at the museum's Acton Depot.

Billy Brown
of London Town

The safest travelling in town
Is not too good for Billy Brown
He's much too sensible and knowing
To jump down off a bus that's going,
Especially in blackout hours
Or when the kerb is wet with showers.
On these occasions Billy B
Goes by the slogan 'Wait and See'.

Printed for
London ⊖ Transport

Above: Annoying advice for bus passengers in the blackout from Billy Brown of London Town, 1940.
Left: The first bus casualty of the Blitz, Mornington Crescent, September 1940. The passengers and crew had taken refuge in a public shelter but eleven residents in this terrace were killed.

difficult with the trams and Underground when trackwork and tunnels were hit. Buses could always be diverted, though nearly 200 LT road vehicles were destroyed by enemy action and many more were badly damaged. Wartime bus travel could be grim and inconvenient but Londoners were pleased, and often surprised, to see this aspect of everyday life maintained. It was a tremendous morale booster.

Did you know?

Buses damaged in air raids often ran with windows missing or boarded up. In September 1940, when the Blitz began, London Transport improvised by glueing fishnet on the side windows to protect them from splintering. This was an effective solution, but the drawback was that passengers could no longer see out of the windows to identify their stop. Inevitably, they started peeling back the corners, prompting the appearance of admonitory notices featuring cartoonist David Langdon's annoying little character Billy Brown of London Town, offering advice in rhyming couplets, such as, 'I trust you'll pardon my correction, that stuff is there for your protection.' Passengers would often scrawl their own retorts. A panel poster on bus stops offering advice on how to hail a bus in the blackout featured Billy intoning, 'Face the driver, Raise your hand, You'll find that he will understand.' One reported response was, 'He'll understand all right, the cuss, but will he stop the blinkin' bus?'

By October 1940 so many buses were out of action through air raid damage that London Transport had to appeal to regional bus operators for assistance. The response was excellent and by the end of the year 468 provincial buses belonging to fifty-one different operators had arrived in London on loan. They added a range of different liveries to the drab wartime capital alongside the familiar London Transport red: green from Exeter, blue and grey from Leeds and a striking blue and white from Hull. The last of the provincials went home in

Four buses burnt out and destroyed by fire after Croydon garage was hit by incendiaries in May 1941.

June 1941, and when subsequent German bombing was directed against new regional targets, London Transport was able to offer 334 of its own buses to help other UK cities.

London Transport 'carried on' and kept the capital going through six difficult years of war when civilians and military personnel were both carried and sheltered across the city. It also made a major contribution to the war effort through its workshops, building bomber aircraft instead of new buses and preparing tanks and landing craft for the invasion of Europe. Much of this vital work was done by newly recruited women who had little or no previous engineering experience.

A large number of women were taken on again as uniformed conductors, who now became generally known as 'clippies', and as garage staff where they cleaned and maintained buses. Some of them were even allowed to drive buses, but only within and between garages when the vehicles were empty. There was no agreement about training women to become bus drivers or inspectors until thirty years later when equal opportunities legislation began to change the work environment.

When the war ended in 1945 it had taken a considerable toll on staff and services. The air raids had killed 426 road and rail staff, with nearly 3,000 injured. A vast amount of repair work to London Transport's bombed or neglected infrastructure was necessary and there was a desperate shortage of buses at a time when passenger numbers were at an all-time high and growing. Reconstruction began almost immediately but it was clear that a long period of post-war austerity lay ahead.

Above left: Evening travel in the blackout was hazardous for passengers and difficult for drivers. London Transport's posters took on a new role offering travel advice and safety warnings, often with a humorous touch.
Above right: Conductor Mrs M. J. Morgan of Athol Street garage, Poplar, who was quietly heroic when her bus was caught in an air raid, bundling four children under the seats. This poster by Eric Kennington is one of six portraits of London Transport staff who 'saw it through' on the Home Front.

To save petrol and diesel in wartime, 160 buses were converted to run on producer gas generated in anthracite-burning trailer units. The buses were slow and unreliable, and the experiment was abandoned when the supply of imported fuel improved.

The Victory Parade in the Mall, 8 June 1946. London Transport entered a pair of RT-types, its final pre-war bus design, seen here passing the King and Queen on the royal dais. Post-war bus delivery would not begin until 1947.

Chiswick colour scheme for the elegant RT-type bus, designed in 1939 with AEC but not put into mass production until 1947 because of the war.

9

Recovery and Stagnation: The 1950s and 1960s

London Transport was nationalised in 1948, becoming the London Transport Executive (LTE), a single division of the British Transport Commission, which was also responsible for British Railways. Under direct government financial control and lacking the dynamic pre-war leadership of Ashfield and Pick, the LTE struggled to find a way forward. London Transport was carrying more passengers on its road and rail services in the late 1940s than ever before, but did not have the resources to properly complete its pre-war modernisation plans. Housing, the new National Health Service and rebuilding other key industries took priority over London's transport needs.

The LTE placed large orders with both AEC and Leyland for an improved post-war version of its RT-type bus but the rate of delivery was slow. Worn out pre-war vehicles were being withdrawn from service faster than new buses could be introduced. It had already been decided to use new diesel buses rather than trolleybuses to complete the tram replacement programme. There were no further extensions to the trolleybus network and the remaining tram routes were closed down between 1950 and 1952.

Did you know?

Mass production of the RT did not start until 1947, when valuable lessons in the standardisation of components learned while LT built Halifax bomber aircraft during the war were incorporated in the post-war design, designated the RT3. Nearly 7,000 buses of the RT family were completed by two engine and chassis builders (AEC and Leyland) and six body builders to give London Transport the world's largest standardised bus fleet by the early 1950s.

RTs were sent on a European tour in 1950 to promote the upcoming Festival of Britain, and later went to the US and Canada. This was the period when the red double-decker became an internationally recognised symbol of London, rapidly recovering from the gloom and devastation of the Second World War.

The first bus to replace trams. A new RT-type leaving the former Wandsworth tram depot over the disused tracks at the entrance, September 1950.

Standardising the fleet. All but one of the eighteen vehicles at Victoria bus station in 1953 is from the post-war RT family.

Stockwell bus garage, completed in 1952, with RT and RTL buses. It had the largest expanse of roof without intermediate support anywhere in Europe. Stockwell is now a heritage-protected listed building and still in everyday use.

London Transport's new overhaul works at Aldenham, completed in 1957. The bodies of the RT family buses could be removed from one chassis and returned to another after steam cleaning and overhaul.

London Transport concentrated its limited resources on research and development in the 1950s, particularly in bus engineering. A huge new bus overhaul works was opened at Aldenham, on the edge of north London, where the enormous scale of London Transport's bus operations could best be appreciated: 1,800 staff were employed to turn out more than fifty completely overhauled buses every week.

Did you know?

An ingenious new roll ticket machine was introduced on London buses from 1953. Conductors had been using the Bell Punch system since the 1890s, carrying a rack of variously coloured tickets representing each fare value in the complicated system. A punched ticket was the passenger's receipt after payment, and the punched confetti in different colours indicated the fares collected, and was a way of checking on the conductor's takings.

The Gibson machine was invented by the superintendent of the London Transport ticket works in Brixton. The conductor could set a dial and turn the handle to print off a ticket to any fare value on the blank ticket roll carried inside. The Gibsons were heavy, and had to be worn by the conductor on a harness, but they were hardy and easier to use than the rack and Bell Punch. They became a unique feature of London buses for the next forty years.

The Gibson roll-ticket machine, introduced in 1953, was unique to London Transport.

In 1954 the prototype Routemaster (RM) bus was unveiled, an advanced diesel bus developed by London Transport to replace the trolleybus. Its unbeaten combination of robust practicality and elegant styling were to make the RM a much loved and long-lived icon of the city. But as the production models entered service from 1959, ousting the electric trolleybus completely by 1962, LT was facing new problems on the streets.

Production of the Routemaster by AEC began in 1958. This is the standard sixty-four-seat bus but there is also a lengthened seventy-two-seat (RML) version and Green Line coaches (RMC and RCL).

Did you know?

The Routemaster project was a design and engineering challenge for Bill Durrant, London Transport's chief mechanical engineer (road services), and his team. The new bus had to be within the statutory dimensions then current (27 ft 6 in. long and 8 ft wide) and no heavier than the RT but carry more passengers. The solution lay in the use of lightweight aluminium alloy throughout and integral construction, which means that there is no separate chassis.

The RM has a metal-frame body with a 'stressed skin' and does not need a chassis to give it structural strength. Assembly involves simply bolting the body to separate front and rear running units instead. The whole vehicle was designed for close precision mass production using jigs to turn out identical parts. Driver and passenger comfort was also important. The RM had the first warm air heating system and was given independent front suspension and coil springs with shock absorbers. These were already standard features on cars but were an innovation for buses, which had traditional leaf springs. All this gave the RM a ride quality equivalent to most saloon cars in the 1960s. Power-assisted steering and an automatic gearbox also made it an easier bus to drive.

Newly delivered Routemasters are prepared for their first day replacing trolleybuses from Poplar Depot, November 1959. In less than three years LT's road services were all handled by diesel buses. Electric trolleybus services ended in 1962.

Since the peak in the late 1940s, passenger use of the red central area services had been in almost continuous decline, for reasons largely outside London Transport's control. The reduction in off-peak leisure travel was particularly marked. Sales and rentals of television sets went up, particularly for the Queen's Coronation in 1953 and again after the introduction of ITV in 1955. Londoners were staying in with their new home entertainment rather than going out to the cinema or a football match by bus.

Car ownership in London increased rapidly once wartime petrol rationing ended in 1950, and more than doubled in the next ten years. This private motoring boom was a double problem for London Transport as it meant fewer passengers and poorer bus services because of growing traffic congestion. The various traffic management schemes introduced in central London at this time – one way streets, flyovers, underpasses and parking meters – did little other than to shift the jams from one pinch point to another, and was of no benefit to buses. Bus lanes only came in gradually from 1968. Congestion, both in central London and the busier suburbs, slowed buses down to speeds little better than those in horse bus days. The comfort of the new Routemasters was no compensation for an increasingly slow and unreliable service.

The public lost confidence in bus services, particularly after a major strike over busmen's pay in 1958 left London with no buses on the streets for seven weeks. There was also a serious shortage of bus operating staff in the 1950s which LT tried to address by taking on more women as conductors and later by direct recruitment from Ireland, Malta and the Caribbean, which continued into the 1960s. Unfortunately this did not solve the staff shortage problems on the buses, which got even worse in the 1970s. Amazingly, women were not allowed to become bus drivers in London until 1974.

Buses trapped in afternoon rush hour traffic at 4.45 p.m., Elephant & Castle, 1966, when no bus-only lanes existed in London.

The first flat-fare 'Red Arrow' express bus route for commuters at Victoria, 1966. To move as many passengers as possible over short distances, these AEC Merlin single-deckers were designed as 'standee' vehicles with very few seats.

The number of passengers carried on London Transport's road services continued to fall, from 3,955 million in 1948 to 2,485 million in 1962. Ever since the merger of the LGOC and the Underground Group in 1912, it had always been the buses that produced most of the money. This deterioration in income therefore struck a mortal blow at the financial viability of the whole undertaking. With operating costs rising and revenue falling, bus services were about to start losing money in the 1960s.

10
Decline and Renaissance: 1970–2000

From 1 January 1970 financial and broad policy control of London Transport was transferred to the Greater London Council (GLC). It was logical to put London's public transport under the authority responsible for strategic planning. London Transport had always been expected to cover its operating costs through fares revenue and contribute to new capital expenditure met by loans or direct support from the Government.

By the late 1960s this funding formula was no longer working as the fall in revenue income had begun to require an annual subsidy. Inevitably, the GLC was soon looking for ways to minimise this subsidy yet at the same time trying to tackle the capital's growing transport problems. Political influence over London Transport became more evident during the 1970s. As political power at the GLC changed hands, from left to right and back again, support for buses ebbed and flowed. Labour administrations broadly favoured public transport, whilst Conservatives advanced priorities for private motorists, but neither had a consistent strategy. This shifting commitment fragmented policy and practice for development of the bus network. At the same time, London Transport's own management was weak and indecisive, failing to respond creatively to the congestion and competition from the private car, or to work in effective partnership with either politicians or town planners. The transport authority, which had started life as a dynamic and forward-looking organisation, had become slow and reactive, no longer setting the pace in urban transport management.

Driver-only operation could save considerably on staff costs but had always been strongly opposed in London, particularly by the transport unions. The traditional layout and open

Daimler Fleetline DMS-type rear-engined one-person-operated buses on the first OPO route through central London, 1971.

back of the Routemaster made this physically impossible with existing double-deckers. In the late 1960s other large cities like Glasgow and Birmingham were investing in front-entrance buses like the Leyland Atlantean for one person operation (OPO). By contrast, London hung back and made only timid trials with a few borrowed Atlanteans and new single-deck buses on selected routes. The much-trumpeted 'Bus Reshaping Plan' of 1966 turned out to be a damp squib, with the purchase of 'off the peg' bus designs forced on London Transport by the terms of new government bus grants.

The first front-entrance double-decker for London designed for cost-saving one person operation was an adaptation of the Daimler Fleetline, a design widely used elsewhere in the country. It was launched by London Transport as the 'Londoner' in 1971 but the name never stuck and the new DMS-type buses became one of the least successful vehicle types ever used in the capital. They were unreliable in London's stop-start traffic and London Transport's engineers and mechanics were unable to deal with overhauls in the established 'flow line' procedure at Aldenham because the bus bodies could not be removed from their chassis. Progress was slowed by poor short-term decision-making at a political and managerial level, which frustrated operations from the garages.

Early experiments with pay as you board fare collection using self-service machines and turnstiles were a disaster. The turnstiles took up a lot of space, would jam easily and were impossible to negotiate with a bag or a pushchair. The alternative was to pay the driver, but you were expected to have the right change available. This was also the period when Londoners were struggling to get used to the new decimal currency introduced in 1971. On many of London's busier routes conductors were retained on new front-entrance buses that were being delayed by long waits at stops, while the driver tried to issue tickets to a queue of boarding passengers.

The unique experimental front-entrance, rear engine version of the Routemaster, FRM1, built in 1967, suggests that London Transport would have followed provincial design trends itself had it been allowed to do so, but with a better quality product. But at the time London Transport could not afford a rigorous research and development programme to come up with its own new OPO bus. Going it alone would have been expensive as the FRM would probably

The sole prototype front-entrance, rear-engine Routemaster bus, built using 60 per cent standard RM parts in 1967. It was never developed for mass production.

not have found sales outside London, a problem encountered by the original Routemaster, which was only bought by one provincial operator. The FRM did not go into production, although ironically the traditional crew-operated RM outlived all the 'off the peg' designs bought by London Transport to replace it.

Did you know?

The last Routemasters soldiered on in regular service until 2005, nearly fifty years after their introduction. By the 1990s most of those still in use had been given new engines and fully refurbished internally. They were finally pensioned off because they no longer met modern access requirements. Their longevity was astonishing considering their life expectancy had originally been put at fifteen years! At the time of writing, a heritage Routemaster route survives in central London with seasonal bank holiday and weekend operation. Old age and nostalgia have endowed the bus with cult status, and there are many in use as private hire buses available for weddings and other functions. It still appears on postcards along with the black cab as an icon of London.

Country bus and Green Line services were transferred to the National Bus Company in 1970 because they were operating outside the GLC area. Even before the political battles of the early 1980s over fares subsidy led to London Transport's removal from GLC control and private sector involvement in operations, there were moves to break down the monolithic structure of the organisation. The remaining central bus operations were reorganised in 1979 into eight bus districts.

Female inspector and driver, 1976. This was only two years after Jill Viner, London Transport's first woman driver, was appointed in 1974.

The Transport Act 1985 brought about bus deregulation throughout the UK, which opened up local bus operation to private operators. In London a completely different model was used from the rest of the country. The Transport Act enabled the privatisation of London bus services managed by an arm's-length subsidiary of London Transport called London Buses. This contracted out the operation of bus services but still determined service levels, routes, frequencies and fares within the public sector.

With the change from a central operating authority to a series of smaller private companies responsible for route operation and all aspects of bus engineering and maintenance, there was no prospect of a return to large-scale standardisation of vehicles. In a sense, the strictly London bus story ended with the Routemaster as the last bus to be designed specifically for the capital by London Transport and to be built in London by AEC and Park Royal coachworks.

But what appeared to be a process of fragmentation and decline for the London bus had some unexpected results. If the first generation of new buses bought 'off the peg' from manufacturers did not measure up to London Transport's traditional high standards, by the 1990s the quality and reliability of new buses had improved considerably. After a brief and bewildering variety of brash colour schemes from new operators that almost sent London back to Victorian times, there was a reassuring return to red as the principal livery for all buses, with a prominent roundel on every vehicle. There was also a much better response to the needs of passengers, particularly at local level.

DISCOVER YOUR
Walthamstow
LOCAL.

From November 19th, wherever you live in the Chingford, Walthamstow or Leyton areas, your bus service will have a new look. New routes, new midibuses and a new service that is designed to fulfill your travelling needs.
Some routes will no longer run and will be replaced by new routes. Others are being changed.

Details of the changes in your area are available in a leaflet that will be coming through your door or from Walthamstow Central Bus Station and Newsagents where you get your Bus Pass from November 14th.
Complete details and timetables for individual routes will be available on the relevant bus from November 19th.

PANEL 9BT

⊖BUS

A LONDON TRANSPORT SERVICE

By 1998 all single-deckers in London were low-floor accessible models, some of which could 'kneel' at bus stops to allow easy access for buggies and wheelchairs. All new buses also had automatic ramps for wheelchair access. The use of frequent midibuses on new local routes instead of infrequent double-deckers improved many services. Vehicle types ranged from midibuses with a capacity of forty, to double-deckers with a capacity of eighty-seven. By the late 1990s, effective service changes with shorter routes had improved reliability and contributed to the first sustained upturn in passenger numbers since the 1940s.

Restructuring monolithic London Buses for the local and suburban market in the 1980s. In Walthamstow this meant using Leyland Titan double-deckers on some services with midi-bus 'hoppas' on short local routes, 1988.

Low-floor buses were an important development in the 1990s. This Dennis Dart 'kneels' at stops to provide better access for all and particularly for wheelchairs and buggies.

Converting to hybrid diesel-electrics in London under TfL and Mayoral governance, highlighted here with special leaf graphics. Trafalgar Square, 2011. (Author)

11

A Way Forward: The Twenty-First-Century London Bus

The return of local government to London in 2000, with the creation of the Greater London Authority (GLA), heralded a renaissance in bus travel. Elected as first Mayor of London was the opinionated Ken Livingstone, whose tenure as leader of the GLC (1981–6) had been abruptly cut short when Margaret Thatcher abolished it after the 'Fares Fair' battle over transport subsidies.

Livingstone made Transport for London (TfL), the new organisation responsible for administering travel networks in the capital, very accountable and transparent. He was elected with a promise to improve London's transport and made significant changes, particularly on the buses. The Mayor pushed through cheaper fares and free travel for the young and old and allowed a revolution that produced the congestion charge, considerable increases in bus volumes and larger vehicles to deliver them.

London's bus network remains unique in the mainland UK in that it is still regulated and gets substantial financial support from public funds, whereas nearly everywhere else bus services have seen a significant decline both in provision and usage. The London model has enabled TfL to plan, procure and manage a network of services in a consistent and co-ordinated manner. Along with adequate funding and close, collaborative working with other organisations, this has led to increased levels and quality of service, together with growing patronage.

Hydrogen fuel cell buses with only water vapour emissions have been operated since 2011. The hydrogen tanks can be seen on the roof. (Wikipedia Commons)

Bus operators compete for contracts to provide specified services for up to seven years. They are monitored and rewarded for exceeding defined targets to improve the service to passengers. Their role is crucial to the current and future success of bus transport in London. The tendering and contracting arrangements are designed to deliver value for money, balancing the expectations of passengers against the cost of improvements. TfL, for its part, is committed to promoting fair and sustained competition to provide bus services in a market that is dynamic and changing.

The Continental articulated bus, used since the 1970s in many European cities, was introduced to London in 2002. The chosen vehicle was a lengthened version of the Mercedes Citaro, already widely used throughout Europe. Its appearance in London coincided with the announcement that the last Routemasters were to be replaced with these single-deck artics. Each 'bendy bus' as they became known, could carry 140 passengers, many of them standing, which was twice the capacity of an RM. They were also fully accessible, with three pairs of doors, which allowed open boarding and easy exit. However, they were open to fare dodging, caused congestion at road junctions and were a threatening presence on the streets for cyclists. Londoners did not take to them.

However, in the early twenty-first century, London became the only place in Britain where bus travel was actually growing rather than declining. TfL invested in new low-emission buses as part of a policy to manage the city's streets sustainably and encourage use of public transport, walking and cycling. Boris Johnson, the next Mayor of London in 2008, had promised in his manifesto that the artics would be 'dispatched to some Scandinavian airport' and within three years they had all been withdrawn and transferred for service elsewhere by their owners, from Manchester to Malta.

Articulated 'bendy buses' at Victoria, 2005. These proved very unpopular in London and were removed on Mayoral instruction after a competition to find a new bus design for London.

New Routemasters in Regent Street, 2015. A worthy successor to the original Routemaster as a new style icon for London. (Author)

Did you know?

Mayor Johnson announced a plan soon after his election in 2008 to give London a new bus which would properly succeed the late, lamented Routemaster with something specially designed and distinctive that could aspire to its iconic status as a recognised

symbol of the city. This was a masterful, though ultimately rather expensive, exercise in Mayoral populism. At a competition launch designers and manufacturers were encouraged to come forward with radical proposals for the New Bus for London. Many of the entries

A classic Routemaster on heritage route 15, followed by an accessible hybrid New Routemaster on the full service route strand, 2015. (Author)

were just that and ultimately vehicle builders Wrightbus of Ballymena, Northern Ireland, were paired with designer Thomas Heatherwick, who was about to provide the torch design for the 2012 London Olympics.

The outcome was a stunning new bus design which incorporated modern features, such as hybrid diesel-electric drive and full easy access via three doors and two staircases, with an authentic feel for London bus tradition. The interior has the welcoming ambience of the original Routemaster, with a similar maroon colour scheme and specially designed seating moquette. The curved rear staircase has a long glass window that echoes the look of the 1920s 'Nulli Secundus', the NS-type. When the first buses entered service in 2012 they even had conductors (customer assistants), whose role was to welcome passengers rather than take their fare (payment now being by contactless or Oyster card). The New Bus for London had no proper name at first and was widely known as the 'Boris bus'. Appropriately, it soon became officially the New Routemaster, setting a new style and standard for London double-deckers. 1,000 New Routemasters are now in service.

Today there are more than 9,000 buses at work in London on 675 routes, far more than in the 'heyday' of London Transport. London now has the largest low-emission bus fleet in Europe. More than 3,000 of them are hybrid diesel-electric vehicles and many more are being retro-fitted with cleaner engines. Hydrogen fuel cell buses that produce no emissions at all have been operating one route through central London since 2010 and are now being used elsewhere. The first service use of single-deck battery electric buses started in 2013 and double-deckers will follow. Between 700 and 800 new low-emission buses are being introduced every year and diesel-only buses are being phased out altogether. This is part of TfL's 'Healthy Streets' strategy that has seen the introduction of an ultra-low emission zone in 2019 and continuing moves to reduce the serious air pollution in the city.

A clean all-electric battery-powered single-decker at London Bridge, 2016. Double-deckers will follow. Is this the future power for London buses? (Author)

New Routemasters in
Whitehall, 2015. (Author)

Annual bus journeys have risen to around 2.4 billion passengers, an almost continuous rise over the last twenty years. There are now more bus passengers carried than in any year since 1959, with a rise of 70 per cent between 2000 and 2015. London has, once again, by far the best and most extensive bus service in the country and other cities in the UK look on it with envy.

On board and in the streets, a digital revolution has been taking place. In 2012 contactless payment using credit and debit cards was introduced on London buses. The take-up was so good that by 2014 it was possible to eliminate cash fares on buses altogether.

Another social change came with information provision. iBus is a radio and Automatic Vehicle Location (AVL) system for buses. It ensures that service controllers at garages know the exact location of every bus fitted with the system at all times. Using a combination of technologies, including satellite tracking and global positioning (GPS) data transfer, iBus keeps track of where London's buses are, allowing bus controllers to regulate services and make them more reliable.

Thanks to on-board 'next stop' audio-visual announcements, passengers know where their bus is, even if they are on an unfamiliar route. They also benefit from more reliable real-time information on 'countdown' scrolling digital indicators at some 2,500 bus stops, giving the expected arrival times of each bus on different routes. With TfL making all its real-time bus data freely available, it was soon possible to deliver this information into the palm of the traveller's hand through apps on a smartphone.

So in 2019 London's bus passengers can access helpful information about services on their mobiles both before and during a journey. They are carried on the UK's youngest, most accessible and environmentally cleanest bus fleet twenty-four hours a day. It is a far cry from George Shillibeer's modest start 190 years ago and can certainly match Ashfield and Pick's heyday at London Transport in the 1930s.

London Buses have recovered their drive for continuous improvement, which was dwindling fast in the 1970s and 80s. The current Mayor Sadiq Khan, the son of a London bus driver himself, and Transport for London are now focussed on environmental sustainability and safe, healthy city transport for the future in which the latest ultra-modern buses will play a major role alongside other transport modes in the city.